No Mud No Lotus

Poems of transformation and grace

Tasha Dagenais

ISBN-10: 1725923467
ISBN-13:978-1725923461

Dedication:

For Pepe, I will always miss you, I will always love you. I hope you're proud of me.

To all my guides and angels, I trust you're here. I feel your love and hear your messages. Thank you for being patient with me.

And for Hilary Lange, because you truly listen and help me when I feel helpless.

Contents:

#1. Remedy

Heart medicine is
Grass weed with pink flowers
Reaching toward a gray sky
Clouds, heavy with rain
Constipated with anticipation.
I'm a ghost laying spread eagle
On the clean earth
Delighted to be green
To be nature again, at last.

#2. The Spector of a Man

How to navigate the spiral
of man's soul descending:

He said, I feel as though I'm coming apart at
the seams
As if I'm seeing the Spector of myself before
I'm dead.

I cradle his face in my hands,
nuzzle the top of his bald head
Gift him butterfly kisses,
And wait,
in case he's more to say.
This separation of self is his alone
I can only be midwife to his evolution
For as long as I'm invited.
But have no claim.
He is not mine, not yet.

#3. Church Wood

A part of me you carry
Is a child of climate science.
An earthier Christian might
Look like a pagan.
A skeptical soul will
Mistake ritual for petty syntax.

Flux is deeply unsettling
Hey, I get it:
Church evokes a history of
Sleepy lecture halls
Geology 101,
Inherited worldview
Built on assumption
That our spinning blue planet
Is stable
Climate, more or less a theory
To take or leave.

Wake up Monkeys!
No whiz-bang solution
technology substitute
For confronting the messy side

of being human.

We are not smarter than nature.

Take your psychedelic trips

Do your recovery work

And at the end of the day

Sure enough, a body poetic

Remains wrapped in hemlock

All thorny like an angry rose

But self-protective

Coded in ancient florals

Offering love

To the deserving

To the eyes wide open enough

To be grateful

For a canopy of trees

Secret fresh water lakes

Rolling hills

Wetlands and

Sacred aloneness

Earth speaking and people listening

To each other as if

For the first time.

#4. Coffee for One

No contact Tuesday

And Coffee for one

a single flower pushing its way through the cracks.

Reminds me that

In the end I mean you no harm.

#5. A Frenchman in America

My mind swims with thoughts of you
Who never let me forget that I was your
Favorite.
I drew stars and you turned them into
people, Penciling in little hands and feet,
adding wide light-filled grins.

You taught me to recognize Daisies,
Tiger Lilly, Alfalfa,
How to use Mint, Sage, and Chive for
Healing.

You reminded me I am more than a wish
I am the potential of my wishes
To be fulfilled.

We walked the cornfields side by side
Played a game of picking our walking sticks
I pretended I was a hobbit and you a wizard.

You spoke beautiful French
Of which I understood not a word
Beyond the musical rhythm.

I remember homemade root beer

And how you always had deli cheese at your
house

While at my house we had plastic tasting
American

In radioactive yellow color.

I remember the first time

I heard the words Cancer and lung.

I don't visit the old house anymore

But went there to find your ghost,

long after the funeral.

And I imagined your ghost,

a short stout French Canadian

Limping on tired knees,

hoisting a twisted wooden cane

Through the dry tall field grass

Before the farmers came back to till the soil

and plant new corn.

Your Spector marching in step with my heart.

#6. Coffee shop Gazing

She should have been writing her stories and
her little bits of scattered thoughts, all
mixed and shaken like a blended cocktail.
Instead, time out. Drive back again to the
rustic little coffee shop on the corner of
Route 101 and the Rectory school Campus. It
was the middle the nowhere really. But a
nowhere of calming thick oak barn doors
converted into quaint small town charm. Rusty
hinges and chipping paint, the same customers
as devoted to coffee as the puritans were to
church. They wear the same ghostly expression
except when exchanging polite half-moon smiles
of hello. She sits in the back near the piano
and the stage, a harmless unassuming admirer.
Someday she'll find the nerve to
say…something.   In the distance, through the
paneled window she views an unspoiled New
England farm cottage. Narrow and white with
black shutters. Unchanged by a hundred
passing years and seasons. The scene invokes
peace, similar to taking a pill for quieting
the seething worry that blazes behind sad
eyes. She is only bearable to herself when
she is working, putting her mind on the page,
going inward, taking the canary yellow walls
of her favorite haunt with her into the
underworld. And that is why she comes here
with note book and curiosity. It's all the
same except for the slow daily shift of
customers chatter and house specials. No
matter her struggles whether a sneeze or
catastrophe, inevitably she'll be found
sipping London Fog Earl Gray tea and gazing
outside from inside the coffee shop like a

figure in a painting, like a distant
apparition.

#7. Antelope Run

Destination; anywhere but the city.

We found ourselves drawn into

Historic mountains of New Hampshire where

The road, cutting through walls of ancient rock,

Took us to Antelope Run.

Population; three hundred forty two.

Fresh air perfumed with pine and bark

Transported our minds and then we saw

The motel sign that read:

Feels Like Home.

Local artwork tells the story of how people

Live here and why. A barefoot boy fishing over the side of a bridge, the sidewalk farmers market

And a hunter taking aim at grazing deer.

Breakfast at Pepper's Diner.

Olive, our waitress,

Is thirty five, tall, slender and kind.

She has deep brown owl eyes.

Olive says to us, "Welcome to Pepper's, grab a booth,

make your selves comfy and I'll be back."

She sings her words like a mother

And I want to move here and stay insulated

In towering pines, the scent of maple syrup
each morning

And befriend Olive, eat every meal at
Pepper's, stay forever

In Antelope Run, disconnected from the city's
distractions.

#8. The Break-up

I asked you not to leave that day.

You couldn't have left in a crueler way,

in silence, only the click of the door
shutting.

I never felt so precious and never felt so
empty.

If only our love had grown bolder

At the sight of blood, embryo,

The forever to be memory of dead baby.

You went back home to someone waiting

You pulled her close, pretended and lied.

You acted like you had been out creating

But you twitched behind the façade.

Licking my wounds and getting strong,

life without you seemed like fate mistaken.

When love became disaster, my heart shattered

I was left to love myself and that mattered.

#9. 4th of July

A cottage, Alexander's lake house.
Bare flesh in bath warm water.
Just a party of friends on the lake.
Youth and dreams, dancing on sand,
We told each other we'd meet at the big ocean
Every summer to swim in the salty indigo.

But as years passed, time slipped like sand
Through clenched fists as we swam and sank
With our legends, our children, our loves
And floated as we tended the watery tides
Of life's changes.

We married, scattered, watered
Our gardens, painted our houses white
And survived our losses
In moments that weathered our characters.

Comrades in the human experience
Some of us learned to walk alone
Some of us gave birth to blue babies
Or hung ourselves on our troubles
Never moved to bigger waters but

But we met each 4th of July
on Alexander's lake.

#10. Soldiers on the Home Front

I'm a raging warrior of soul.
Fighting my own wars while he is away
Rise, rise up and march all soldiers.

Who else will tend the babies when sick or
cold?
We women struggle at home and pray.
I'm a raging warrior of soul.

I might fight with my heart alone
While missing him and feeling I might give
way.
Rise, rise up and march all soldiers.

Generals of hearth and home,
stop seeking your husbands.
I'm a raging warrior of soul.

He will return from war to hold me
So I'll worship our daughter as we play.
Rise, rise up and march all soldiers.

His absence left us with a giant hole.
We ache for his return this May.

I'm a raging warrior of soul.

Rise, rise up and march all soldiers.

#11. The Cross Out

Random

Quotation of the week.

No other

Various opinions

Breaking ground.

Ultimately

Pressure to consume

Another layer.

Influence

Instituted

Robbery.

Walked around

Seeking information,

Demanding money.

The suspect

In the end indicated this to me.

#12. The High and Low of Place

Profile of a busy- airy town:
Villas built on sand and shells,
Victorian castles on Rocky Mountains.
A place of historic celebrity
Where people gather for firewater
Celebrations and new age spell casting.

I yield church in a nature walk, see exotic
Birds, and flowers of unnamed colors.
In this place beauty shares its path
With antique dealers, bars and billiards,
Community halls and family YMCA's.

The town's history began with the wolves
Until the early ranchers came and killed
Every last one. Becoming themselves,
The infectors. Garbage piled up and people
Wandered like hungry ghosts, falling into
Cracked pavement and addiction.

But time does heal most wounds:
Today, palm trees grow beside waterfalls,
The sights settle the town's restless

Daydreams. In place of littered streets rose
Twenty four hour spas, cheap restaurants,
A casino on the road to the canyon.

Here in this corner of the world
We blend the high and the low
And I continue to dance between extremes
Trying to find my place, my preference
In a reality of too many choices.

#13. Dawning Light

A lonesome August morning walk,
Except for your ghost, faithfully beside me.
I'm still shaking off
the last knock upside the head,
delivered in a long awaited letter,
written to disarm me.

My feet are cut up from
Walking on the eggshells
You laid over my path,
And my muscles are weaker from
Holding my boundaries;
Protecting this fortress of stick and stone.

Who will match my heart now?
I know the truth of you
Considering how
Clock time and 3 dimensions
Are disappearing before my eyes

Not a single familiar face in sight.
I'm holding out for the angels,
Ascended masters and

To hell with blood.

#14. Iris's Enchanted Summer

Iris has decided against madness
At least for today, no negotiations
With her own mind
About sanity.
She is a gathering harvest
Of Indian summer dreams

Iris opens the car windows, and
Welcomes the warm wind combing her hair.
The air isn't hazy, it's soft
The sky isn't a ceiling, its infinity.
A sensation of lushness passes
Through Iris, replacing the usual
Depression. Most days Iris is a dazzling calm
Before noon. A turmoil of mental noise
By 3. And a soul's mercy by 6.

Iris buys organic vodka
Running shoes from Payless
Herbal Hibiscus tea from Vanilla Bean.
One scene molds into another,
A Multi-screen vision of life in motion
Infuses commutes, errands, road trips.

While the spicy dryness of a ripe season
Nudges Iris to spread her wings
Of longing for no more pain.

While the days are greener, bright
With ease and enchanted with
Tiny buzzing- flittering creatures
Iris can heal. She is a gathering harvest
Of Indian summer dreams.

#15. Thank you Mr. Peterson

Did you always want to be a Rock star?

I'm happy for you. Will you be happy for me?

Will we be together nature's goodness

In a Thanksgiving kitchen

And embrace when we meet like soldiers

Who marched and crawled together

Died and resurrected together in mysterious
wood

On distant shores?

I see you now all earthy elegance

And a gratitude runs within, so deep

I can't help feeling the truth of your heart

Lecturing on a neon purple stage.

The attention of 2,300 minds

Hanging on your every word.

You have lifted me from moments of chaos.

You have made me wonder, why not me?

Not in pity, but rather in possibility.

#16. Spell For Revolution

That last bit of summer,
golden with flowers and fading warmth
as the first notes of fall appear.
Dash of sandalwood.
Evening star. Soft pine. Midnight berries
Spellcasting for lawlessness and a revolution
Calling on the Abolition of traditional forms.

#17. Enchanted Moon

Sheets dancing on the clothes line.
Mayhem and anarchy,
Hanging patiently in the night sky
Like the Enchanted Moon.

#18. I Tell the Stars about You

Fuck off with your Pomegranate kisses.

You wear Artful motifs. But no one can hear you.

You could be warm oil. Cedar wood and sage.

Your charm is expression. You Neutralize spheres.

We meet in entryways, dorm rooms, offices.

Voice like silver birch

You're a medley of leaves.

I tell the stars about you.

#19. Night Clouds

A Rustic infusion of sunflower days and warm cedar.

Grapevine and oak drift into Night clouds.

Steam distillation from fir needles

Lend magic to the tranquil mist of mid-week.

Jewel mosaics blend well with late blooms.

Twilight silhouettes welcome the subtle musk

Of ancient prayer and healing touch.

#20. Building Bridges

My Journey is through strength
Thanks to building bridges instead of walls.

I wanted to pass my recovery onto someone
Who would come home with me, make me behave.
No one ever did.

The past is no excuse, it doesn't make it so
Thanks to building bridges instead of walls.

Without being controlled by what others think
of me,
I speak more gently, I'm a little less
defective.
Thanks to building bridges instead of walls

I learned to accept a seed of hope to ease my
days
After swimming in deep waters for so long.

I learned to say no. Then I learned to let go.
Thanks to building bridges instead of walls.

#21. Life Flows

Life flows regardless
Of going to a dry well for water
And summer time won't wait
For a locked heart.
And still somewhere deep
Underground nourishment flows.
Go deeper and dig your grave
If you must. You might find
A journey into darkness
Reveals an untouched river.

#22. Trinity

Moving through a forum
Of features
The father
Son
Holy Spirit
One God in three persons.

Another day competing with thin-spiration
Living in self-maintenance mode
Stuck-on-survive
No longer works
Getting out of my own way
When I stop feeding chaos
When I no longer feel broken
And the healing power of intimacy
To be a trusted servant
to be the wife he deserves.

And I arrive
I pray
to find a new life-out from under
Finally, in a place of safety.

#23. Softness is Yoga

Yoga is more than just a body
making shapes.
With Softness you can slide
Into the stars
you can be
Light beams traveling through
In all directions.
You already are what you are becoming
That is the trick of possibility.

You are the big bang
You are the source
That makes feeling possible.
You open doors to creativity
You came from what you are
Like vapor is water.

You are softness embodied
You are the action of aligning with
The wild nature of universe.
You are third eye opening
When you are able to see others
And can serve with love.

Become moveable
And you can be moved.
Get out of your own way.
You. Are. Spirit.

Decorations aren't necessary
A script is for theater.
Subtract. Use only what you need.
Don't move against yourself
And you'll be free to let potential
Swoop into you.
Easy does it. Quiet the noise inside.
Soft and easy as you go.

#24. Gates of Departure

Goodbye Behavior at an airport
A dried cucumber seed stuck to my heel
I can no longer talk about what I do
Or don't do.

Language doesn't serve me
A cramp squeezes my right eye
Tightens like a rope into my heart.

Emotion catches in my throat
The busyness of shuffling feet
Bottled feelings expanding.
Lives unfolding at gates of departure.

#25. Truth and Coffee

Shuffling forward the in the coffee line.
Fox News deafening in the background.
Delicate beauties in black dresses,
Fall like angels into the door.
High on attractiveness. A rose doesn't need
To do anything to be sacred.

A nurse wearing kitty-cat cartoon scrubs.
A pimple faced realtor in ironed shirt and
tie.
A mother soothing a restless toddler
While bouncing a baby on her hip.
One customer at a time. One transaction.
Another score of speed.
Are we a country that runs on coffee?
Or weariness?
Are we lab rats going back and forth,
to a drugged water bottle?

Maybe we are shuffling together
Toward a new view of each other.
We are dirty water trickling
Down the suffocating drain.

If you're crazy you're a liability
If you're a liability you can't get help.
The game is set so you can't win.
Except defeat. Game over.
Now you can be free. So let go. Let go.
One customer at a time.
One transaction at a time.
I'll have a medium black iced coffee.
Light ice please.

#26. A Friday Prayer

God, please make me an instrument of your blessing.

I will do whatever it takes to let go

Of precious things.

Earth- Air- Water and Fire, help me see your mysterious ways.

I will do whatever it takes

To understand the lessons without alarm or unease.

Spirit of the North Winds, make me an instrument of your peace

I will do whatever it takes

To heal hearts and dry tears.

#27. Fire Dance

Norwegian Inspired symphonic music. Re-mixed-

It's the grieving soul's spirit-

Letting awe be awe, making me believe

In re-birth once again.

No need to shave my head this time.

But a dance around the fire pit on a spicy night-

Highly recommended.

#28. Ode to 12 Steps

One Quote for each new day.
Gems of wisdom jumping
Off the pages at me.
But the person I resented most
Became my best teacher.

I formed a rescue mission
With the angels of my dreams
And calmly, through the river
Grew into myself in service
To the greatest secret of all,
Comfort through living
The serenity prayer.

Sometimes an ending is the hope
Of the very first meeting.

#29. Anonymous Morning

Inhaling the moist soil sweetness
of roughly 6 O'clock in the morning
Angels of promise and renewal
Gathering in a dreamy sunrise
Haloed in fragments of sun light,
filtered through a screen of leafy trees.
Cars idling in driveways as neighbors
wait for their first cup of coffee
To register them as human.
Slow motion, stop motion.
For only a couple more hours
taking time to wave hello.
Because morning is stillness
then speed of pace and thinking
Accelerate and quicken.
I pause in awe, with a hot mug
of black coffee cupped between
creased palms. I give my name back,
surrender my slogans and chose
To dress and move within neutral tones.
Mornings strip me of name and story
For a few precious hours I am
Anonymous. I am free of sorrow,

Free of thought and breathe light.

#30. Unity Science

Entering the center of gravity

The inter-change of my inner and outer worlds

Severed from reality- in a realm beyond reach.

How do I get to that place

Where I can touch him without pushing him
away?

My confusion cowers like a guilty dog.

I want nothing to shine through me

Which reveals false identity.

Who is really keeping their shit together?

People selling advice about keeping your shit
together?

It's all red balloons and party time on the
screens

But the human heart is a spider web,

tangled three dimensional silk traps,

Stronger than steel and as dangerous as lust.

I'm into the unity of all the things, distinct
disciplines

that form a complex whole.

I want to stop overthinking and ride

the infinity belt while I'm in it. Now.

We keep nothing of this world except

the love we make.

#31. Undo the Human, Become the Soul

Inside outside, alone again.
Crushed under a mash-up of oneness,
Philosophy and chatter.
What's keeping him so long?
The savior, the shaman, the star.

Discovering by the day an
Inner light within dark arts.

Think about how many heroes
Are murders. How many holy men
Are crucified after following
The mountain call.

Be aware of the wishes you make
they may not be the best
thing that happens to you,
your own crumbling.
Undo the human, become the soul.

#32. SpeedDating is a Single word

Speed dating is the fast food of sex.
You go all the way in
And fall into your role as
Another link in the think sync struggle.
SpeedDating is a formula
Of express meet and greet.
Speed dating as two words
Is only a generic term for similar events.
It's the fad matchmaking formula
More addictive than nicotine
More attractive than riches
As fleeting as the next orgasm.

#33. The Healing Mirror

You are my healing mirror,

You recruit my better nature.

You see my frown and pledge me truth,

You offer vows outside my safe limits-

That you are here. Real. Consistent.

You provide grace of a witness

To the crazy that leaks despite

My trying to hold it in.

You love me, shadows and all.

Too long I drew a memory of divorce

And the disease of damage

Like the chalk outline of a victim,

As definition of the crimes against me.

But you see right through me

And that is how I can admit

I am powerless against my own mind.

Protected by the flawless truth

That I am lovable despite the damage

Starring back at me.

#34. Goblin Entertainment

I can see the goblin that will Let us down.

His names are depression, rage, fear.

He wants me to think he is many

But he is one: struggle, suffering, Pain, burning.

A mischievous, ugly troll, greedy for creative gold

feeding off the airs of my dreams, whispers stories

of a demon past on the back of my neck. He stalks

over my universe from day break to days end.

"Run rabbit, run", he sneers in my ear.

I am his mortal fun. My Goblin is trickier than

a spider, as famished as a starving wolf.

I spit jokes at the feet to his amusement,

I clown and the Goblin hoots, this is how I take

My power back, make hilarity of reality.

It's easier than it seems, this human life is ridiculous.

#35. Tangentially Iris

Iris calls me drunk. It's 2am. Her sentences come at me like a whip. I catch words like butterflies in a net. Iris has always been pleasure and pain swirled together like a fancy cocktail. She's bored again and googling conspiracies. Iris drinks and dials once a week, when she's grown sick of taking orders from the lord and master. Iris says, everybody has at least one boss, they're answering to the man, the supervisor, corporation, road rules and state laws, tax codes, courts, family, debt. Some think they are free and the rest of us wrong to live week to week for a paycheck. But freedom is a fool's irony. It means they can't see their cages. We are all ruled by the rules of simply being alive. Iris transforms into bitch goddess energy when no one's around to pet her. She finishes a half hour rant, eats a deep sigh and calms. We make a date for coffee at the café with Native American pottery, a player piano, whole leaf tea, a place where gold-dust dances and with that promise of see you later we say goodnight and goodbye for now.

#36. Naked

There is a crack in your orbit
Where all the love leaks out
And romance touches heartache.
There is a crack in your secret
Where all the truth bleeds
And all the lies are naked.

#37. Queens and kings

A woman wants a man's passion most of all.

If she doesn't know that, she's a princess,

not a Queen. A Queen knows the privilege

of riding the loop of infinity

with another soul. A princess will cage a
boy,

means to keep him; but a queen values a
lifetime

of old dear friends. She is kind enough

To let go.

A princess falls in love with tricksters

and fools. Boys not men.

A queen understands the form a choice takes

is deceptive, To the lesson beneath.

A queen knows it's in service to whom or what

a choice is made from within that makes a
king.

#38. Brat

She did it again-Relationship Sin
Guilty before a crime was committed.
A Jealous brat at her best,
corrosive self-awareness.
Identity is short term deterioration.

Soft negatives won't prevent
moods bouncing off one another
Like ping pongs.
The little differences in words uttered,
body tones, gazing into space
a listless lover, so far gone as to never
have been there to begin with.

#39. Wild and Free

When the waking began
I lost the shape
of objects outside nature.
Then form and shade
became fluid.
Next colors diluted
and a grayish blue bruise
Remained.
One tipsy evening
I created a soul
named Shadow
inside my head.
He invokes
The Yankee grit in me
And he's desperate
To leave this
Stale cracker mill town
With its relentless
Sameness.
I could have been
a heart untouched
By illness but I am
Nameless to forces
of season and change.

The cycles continue
With no regard to me,
these are the terms
and conditions
Of aging and damage,
To accept this life
For its organic messiness
And find forgotten power
Within the wild freedom
Of organized chaos.

#40. Imagination Engine

Mastering perception is
Learning to drive a car in reverse
turning your view over, inside-out
upside down, flip creation bottoms up
and remember those who wish to correct
your thinking are wrong too.
I'm full of bullshit, just like you
What do I know? Imagination.
Our minds are engines of creation.
Passion is an unsatisfied companion
It's awake when you thirst for more.

#41. Whetstone

If you want to Learn to float beyond the pain
go to the Whetstone, ask if the blade is sharp
Press harder, circular movements,
wrist and blade control are everything
bare down, press harder, use less and less
pressure. Bare down, press harder, ease up,
less pressure. When you start floating
above the pain, the razor is sharp enough.
Now, where in hell is the Samurai?

#42.   Wounded Healer

August breezes pry warm fingers
around drafty windows, kiss your cheek
caress your feverish forehead.
Your lover's quarrel is with God
Not one doctor in existence
Believes your heart attack was
Caused by long term loneliness
You are now the blind and wounded
Healer.

#43. All You've Got

The ingredients for peace are all around you
but exist to you alone and you aren't sure
you're any more real than a confession without
a witness. A crate of used books, a fresh
water fish tank, borrowed library DVDs you'll
never watch, bitter home-made iced coffee.
You're wrapped in $5 consignment gray & black
cotton, waiting for the modem lights to turn
green despite stacks of unread books and
sunlight still blessing the day in golden
haloes but somewhere close someone has crashed
into a utility pole, and knocked out internet
for miles. Something isn't right in your
world and you can't talk about it. Then the
phone chirps. It's your little brother, not
so little anymore. He's sent you pictures of
your new baby nephew. You wish you weren't an
hour away. You want to be close to another
human body right now. Instead you're thankful
someone remembered you today. You stay with
what you've been given. In a little while
it'll be enough, it's all you've got.

#44. The Toe of Awakening

The toe of awakening is
a complex intersection
of low-income anxiety,
shared space and a moment of silence
in a church basement.
Turns out when she identifies with challenge
anything is possible.
So she counts her blessings
and looks for a hand
to hold before she jumps from the edge
of anger and shame
while flowers grow from her heart
and the blood in her veins
is still warm.
She's busy pondering the dream
But it's clear
something is amiss deep down.
She only wants him to touch her.

#45. For A New Earth

Faith overcomes and anchors the mind

It's too easy to lose sight

Of what a new reality looks like

In this flood of information,

Jumble of values, religious conflict,

Terrorist attacks, arms races,

Nuclear war, refugee crisis,

Social welfare, political chaos.

Does God really exist?

How many Americans Understand?

What it means to live in a military state?

A world beyond differences,

Requires integrated reasoning

For a new earth.

First we befriend the body and then

We forgive, and forgive and keep

Forgiving every single yucky thing

About our lives.

#46. Magic and Moonlight

Iris Wakes at roughly 2am in tangled sweaty
sheets. The dream of skeletal hands reaching
out to her, quickly slipping away. Between one
day and next, between time and space, Iris is
alone in her lavender bedroom.

An unusual moonlight and magic spills in
through the windows, calls to Iris like a
witness to court. Starlight mixes with
earthlight and bounces off heaven's surface
which is all things everywhere of liquid, air,
and flow.

As the moonlight strikes Iris's sorrow, like a
silver elixir a sudden sympathetic twilight of
unearthly wonders spirits all Iris's worries
away and relieves the melancholy that weakens
her knees. She's spellbound by a mellow misty
pale of peaceful uncertainty.

And the strong radiance of soft magic becomes
a weird yellow warmth wrapping itself against
her like one of her Gram's handmade quilts.
Magic and moonlight, a ghostly mother rocking
her child safely into morning.

#47. Sands of Wisdom

A man worships pale blue morning sky.
He's just run miles as if
His life depends on it.
Run his lungs raw,
run to beat himself.
Red sand beneath him,
all around him inside his soul,
Scratching at his desire
an allergic blessing
of ancient wisdom and cosmic truth,
blossoms into skin rash and fever.
He's teased by the French kiss
of a breeze starved
for prayer and advice only
A woman can provide.
He wonders where his angel
has been taken
and how he'll find her.
He worships sand, dessert,
and space as far as he can see.
He must journey from the sacred
Mountains where wisdom will be waiting.

#48. Deeds of a Hero

Are you still my future king, pulling sword from stone?

A blind mystic leading me away from the underworld?

Are you my Greek god, using silk threads to escape danger?

Are you the Great Alexander, successful commander changing the face of a warring world?

Are you undefeatable like Achilles, baptized in mythic water?

Are you Odysseus, grandson of Olympians, and humble with wit, intelligence and skill?

Our remembered heroes are mortal too, they did not try to know why, they just believed and burned and rised like phoenix from the ashes.

#49. Tidal Wave

As summer is ending
Nature seems to be saying
One last burn,
One more stifling Tidal wave.
I'll become salt
Swallowed by the Sea.

#50. Goodbye

The sky the morning you left
Was as pink as my sunburn.
I'm on the mend and bending to
Accommodate uncertainty.
Cruising roundabout the wooded backroads
In my six speed on a Sunday afternoon
And not a single shred of nostalgia
Stirred to lift me from the doldrums.

#51. Ode to Northern Lights

Where the snow glows

Shadowy mountains surround

Unveiling magnetic emerald ribbons

For guardians of the northern regions.

Observers taste cold Velveteen twilight,

Hear their heart's joy thumping a rhythm

With the circus in the atmosphere.

This canvas for heaven's dance

Softens winter's arrival

With azure, violet, and yellow wonders

The sky presents its strange tricks.

Magic is reflected off Icy lakes

And colors swarm the Arctic night.

#52. Decide to Change

I couldn't decide whether to throw a party or get a divorce.

I couldn't decide whether to force solutions or resolve the conflicts within. Confused between the shower and the bath. The house or the apartment, to stay or move far away, tea or coffee, a baby or a puppy.

I couldn't decide between hot truth and white lies. Didn't know what to do about anything or stand with others who saw me as some-thing.

I let wisdom dance alone on the periphery.

This morning's news reported another story of a nine year old boy, gay, bullied, and took his own life. I thought maybe this kid had more courage than I do. Then I prayed God, bless him and change me.

#53. Spirit's Sunrise

A Spirit's sunrise puts to bed
a nightlife of wine and wild delights.
Bird song of a new day,
a blank page, and an open road
awakens me from fast fading dreams
and the morning reaches toward me
asking only that I reach back.

#54. Enjoy the Ride

Swift as glory and goodness
we go into the light.
It's easy when the season tastes sweetest
just before turning to rust.
We think we begin with nothing
We were born blessed
and need to give ourselves permission
to enjoy the ride.

#55. Harvest Spell

Fox dances, Owl hoots invoking the rising
Of Harvest Moon.
The ripest florals soon become mutable shades,
as sweaty afternoons cool to a
crisp calm on the face of frosty mornings.
From the first autumn sunrise to winter's
First icy kiss I am here for another day.
Overnight thousands of frenzied people are
greeted by the soft drum beats of River-fire
Celebrations while the world re-plants itself
Underground and it is up to the people
To remember how beauty can rise from the
Underworld. In the meantime, I am swarmed
by violet floras and red worrisome visuals
Of weather's wilting and summer's song
Going silent.

#56. Humanoid

Sisters' when the voice of your eldest brother
Barks inside your head, know the voice is a
Lie.

Daughters, journey far from your mother's
Nest. Do not return until a Goddess tells you
To.

You never come back to Normal.
You only get a new life and gold dust
Of all the previous ones to remind you that
You get what everyone gets
A human experience.

#57. Time Traveler

I must be a time traveler
Hearing the crunch of gravel driveway I
haven't walked over in decades, the voices of
those whom I loved and are long dead.
Laughter so clear it mine as well be standing
beside me.
I'm haunted by lives I haven't yet lived and
the grasses of my childhood home under my bare
feet. I smell decoration boxes in the farm
house attic, March Daffodils, I taste pea pods
fresh from the garden. I'm listening to
insects buzzing in summer, I'm holding my baby
brother on our green couch in a wood-paneled
living room. I feel his warm sack of a body in
my four year old arms.
I'm being hummed a lullaby and woken in the
middle of the night for alcohol rubs to reduce
fever.
Close my eyes and I can go anywhere in time,
take my senses with me, it's bilocation and
no-one notices the shift. Who I was and what I
could become, are a blink away, adrift between
parallel forever.

#58. Dreamscape

You built your village on red-stained sand.
You fear you'll die waiting for a foreign sun
and heard today that Earth is burning toward a
timeless desert. You don't mind a hard knock
life, an Advil PM daze each night engaging
slumber. Your mission is figuring out what
exactly free-falling means.
Spinning?
Riding the space-time continuum?
Giving up and giving in?
Which story did you wake up in today?
Whose dream did you intrude last night and
who's been trespassing into yours?

#59. Earthquakes Likely

No one's fault but my own
That I trusted you to care for the things I
love above you.
A foolish miscalculation that put me unsteady
on the fractured ground, could be fiction or
truth,
But one thing is certain: Earthquakes are
likely to occur.

#60. Bewitching Hearts

The bewitching season begins with you, so get
steady Pumpkin, and give her your best spiced
kiss of clove and silky white lies.
You're the sweetest seduction she's ever
known. You cast a snake's spell over all who
dwell in your circle because yours is the
shape that provokes wicked thoughts, your
charm is a ruby rose blend of blood-cherries
and steamy bubble-baths.
In contrast she is blue twilight storm,
A witch's brew of mist and moonbeam. Her
allure is cashmere skin, Stage Theater, honey
and whipped vanilla humor. Midnight falls on
her like a guillotine. But you are the
lessoning of hurts, the warm flame of a second
chance. Your enchantments are welcome here
but tread lightly, she is treasure when you
steady her heart against yours.

#61. Deceit

My mind in knots just realized it doesn't want
to die but can't live beside a man who hates
everything I stand for.

He promised me a wish on the evening star. He
doesn't know that his eyes scream what he
cannot say.

Double dealing behind my back and He thinks
not telling me is the same as not lying. The
sound of his breathing is no longer sweet.

#62. Final Goodbye

Our final bow
To an audience of none.
A hush and whimper
Passes between the space
Where we stand apart.
Goodbye carries the weightless
Impact of memories that will
Fade eventually.
It's up to us to make
This moment worth the pain.

#63. We Wave Hello and We Wave Goodbye

Iris asked me why it ends in tears.
It was early September and the loudest night
Of nature's song. A Corus of buzzing,
Chirps and hoots, symphony of howls,
slithering and sweeping.
We were leaning on the hood
of her 1998 Honda Accord, reviewing
love's lies, addiction and awakening
to the things we thought were lost along
the way. Iris is six months sober and doesn't
know how to celebrate a milestone
without drugs and sex.
I said, we wave hello and we wave goodbye.
Yes but why?
I don't know, I guess that's life.

Acknowledgements:

During the composing of this book I've been
especially inspired and motivated by the JRE
podcast, The DTFH, Tangentially Speaking with
Dr. Christopher Ryan, WTF with Marc Maron, The
Aubrey Marcus Podcast, and The Church of
What's Happening Now with Joey Diaz. I'm
Thankful to Russell Brand for helping shift my
perspective around recovery and spirituality.
Thank you Marianne Williamson for your free
weekly live streams, thank you Henry Rollins
for your stories, disciplined energy and
motivation. Thank you Jocko Willink, your
posts are daily lessons in cultivating grit
and never giving up.
Thank you Al-Anon for saving my life more than
once. Thank you The Friends of the Killingly
Public Library for welcoming me. Thank you
Hilary Lange for helping me sort myself out.
Thank you Nick, No matter what happens, you
and me, it's a soulmate thing.

About the author:

Tasha Dagenais is an aspiring poet, writer and yogi. She was born in New England and is the author of *Acquiring Satellites Poems of desire and spirit*.

Made in the USA
Coppell, TX
09 March 2022

74702900R00046